Edge Control for the Soul

Edge Control for the Soul

written by Brianna Laren
artwork by Delmaine Donson

Illustrator: Delmaine Donson

For information about special discounts for bulk purchases, please contact us at info@BriannaLaren.com.
www.BriannaLaren.com

PRINTED IN THE UNITED STATES OF AMERICA

ISBN: 978-0-578-78772-5
(Paperback)

ISBN: 978-0-578-78773-2
(E-Book)

This book is dedicated to every Black woman that has ever been told she is not enough. To every single Black woman that has to shrink herself to fit into spaces that she is constantly reminded weren't built to hold her.
To every Black girl that has been made to feel less than or has to shout to be heard and is then quickly hushed by those that despise her presence.
To every Black boy that has ever been called a thug or made to think that the only way he can make it in this world is to sell his soul.
To every Black man that has ever had to hold in his rage, his hurt, his pain or even his joy just to fit into the chalk outline society has drawn around him.
I see you, I hear you, I am you. I write for you and to you and I love you.

To those who have loved me and inspired me along the way: My parents, my husband, my family and my strong circle of friends. Also, to my sun & my moon, Bam & Bella.

To my dear friends Franklin, Justin, & Jon:
I love you more than words could ever describe. Your mother's memory will live on through you. You are her legacy.

In Loving Memory of:
Mary B Faison
Kathy "Kat" Thompson
Robert Judd
Darius "DJ" Dawson
Donna Barr

feed your soul

I have always been a dreamer, when I was little I had this active imagination that led me to believe I could be and do anything. However, as I grew older my dreams got smaller due to people continuously telling me I needed to be more realistic. I listened and neatly folded my dreams up, placed them in a box and tucked it away in a corner.

I had to find a REAL major & choose a REAL career path so I could make REAL money. However, that didn't work out too well for me. Everything I did lacked purpose & my heart wasn't in it.

So... I found that metaphorical box I had tucked away and dusted it off. I began doing what filled me with joy and purpose... WRITING ... creating stories, characters and content that positively impacts the world.

Has it made me a billionaire, not yet. Will it ever? I don't know and I don't care. I still have a "real job" & that pays the bills but writing... that feeds my soul.

What feeds your soul?

from my soul to yours.
Brianna Laren

for patsi

I don't remember any celebrities I wanted to be like as a child. I just remember wanting the strength of my great-grandmother, Patsi. I remember walking the rugged cement deathtraps DC calls sidewalks with Patsi. Maneuvering my little patent leather shoes through glass, trash, & old gum.

I tiptoed over cracks as if my mother's back depended on it. I held my grandma's hand so tightly her sweat became my sweat & my hand became her hand. I've been in a room filled with cops before all highly trained & armed with guns but I've never felt safer than I did wrapped in my great grandma's arms.

I remember her stories vividly as if they were a play I attended over & over again until I knew each line. I remember the smell of her & her house. If ever I smell something that reminds me of her, my world pauses. I'm a child again sitting on the couch playing in her hair. I'm that little girl again seated on stacked phone books at the kitchen table.

Too small to fit in the adult chairs so there I sit, on phone numbers, names & addresses of people I will never meet. I sit patiently awaiting my grandmas home cooked meal. It's served with love seasoned with hope & paid for with sacrifice.

Her smile was so genuine, her laugh so heartfelt, her words so painfully honest. I couldn't wait to grow up to be like this woman. This woman that raised my grandma , my mom & now me. At that tender age I didn't realize how blessed I was .. but now.. Oh now.. I realize that God loved me so much that He allowed her to live to grow wrinkles & gray hair all so she could be there for me.

Grandma Bacon, your memory will forever be in my heart and will live on through my children and through my children's children.

I believe our journey as black women is, in a lot of ways, very similar to the natural hair journey. The journey of self- discovery, getting to know ourselves, loving ourselves in totality, nurturing our gifts, and showing others how to love us. It all connects.

I told this story through poetry because that is where I can be my most vulnerable. As black women, we have been conditioned to hide and mask our vulnerabilities so they can't be used against us. We have to remain strong and impenetrable at all times but that gets really heavy after a while. You find yourself carrying things you should have let go of a long time ago.

That is why poems, to me, are extremely intimate. I hope sharing the deepest & darkest parts of myself, along with the most beautiful parts will inspire you to let go. My hope is that you will drop the mask, embrace every part of yourself, step into the light and allow the world to see you. But most importantly I hope you grow and thrive.

contents

breakage

breakage

i am not okay
i know i said i was
but i'm not
i lied
i do that a lot

i smile when i want to cry
i can't explain why
i say i'm fine
when i'm really dying inside

it's instinct i guess
to pretend i'm not a hot mess
most days
i am like the junk you shove in drawers
or the crumbs on the floor
you quickly kick away
when company is on the way
to make it appear like you keep your house clean

breakage

oh and i am really good at pretending
like oscar worthy good
and i'm extremely strong
i can carry years worth of baggage
i carry it with honor
and never get tired
except i am
i am damn tired
i don't usually curse
but this moment calls for it

today i heard in a song
"it's okay not to be okay"
and i burst into tears
it was not a cute cry
like not at all
i was a blubbering fool
with the viola snot
except this wasn't a performance

this came with no applause
but it was so freeing because
i could finally drop the act
and cut the crap

i could finally say
i am not okay

manipulation

i thought i knew what depression
looked like
i thought i would recognize it
because i saw it on tv & movies
& read about it in books
i saw it in the faces of those i loved

but no one told me that depression is
like a thief in the night that sneaks
into your home & steals all your valuables

it skips past your flat screen
and goes right for the things that make you,
you
it lurks around waiting for you
to be at your most vulnerable
and slowly begins stealing
things little by little
it is so smooth
and so silent
and so meticulous
that you don't even notice anything is missing at first

a smile here
a laugh there
until you're unable to see
the beauty in anything

manipulation

the little things add up to the big things
the little things are what keep us going
& depression knows that

i thought i knew what depression looked like
but it wasn't just smudged mascara
or nonstop crying

it looked
like
me

like a shell
of who i used to be

wrapped up

i feel trapped in this place
this place that once made me feel safe
makes me feel like i might suffocate
i am struggling for air

my thoughts are jumbled
and my future uncertain
this place that once comforted me
makes me scared and sick to my stomach

it makes me wonder if
it was ever what i wanted or
was i blinded by something else

the paint is chipping
the pictures have fallen off the walls
and the floors creak
it is in dire need of tlc
that i don't have the strength
or the energy to give it

i feel bamboozled
was it always like this?
i am mad at this place for
changing
so rapidly

but maybe it is me that has changed

wrapped up

have i outgrown this place?
i'm a full sized person
in a doll sized house
trying to make it work
forcing myself to fit somewhere
i no longer belong

i don't know
my place in it anymore
i'm not happy here
all the windows but one
are boarded up

it only allows me
the view it wants me to see
no room for interpretation

i am not myself here
i can't hear myself here
i am a ghost
wandering the halls of a
place i can't leave
or can't let go of
not certain which one is true

if i demolish it, will i go too?
if i stay i'm only half of myself
so what is there really to lose?

unraveled

i'm in this dark place
i can't see your face
and i have lost sight of who i am

there is nothing around
i am crying out
but can't hear a sound

somebody
save
me

heat damage

i see your flaws
and i don't care

i see the signs
the flashing lights

i dive in heart first
the common sense
rushes out of me

i see it coming
the worst of it
like a cliche movie
i can guess how it will end
but i watch anyway
because maybe
just maybe... i'm wrong

i ignore sound advice
i hold on 'til the death of it

you split me
to the root
i could have prevented it
stopped it
before you consumed me

but now
it's too late

gelled up

i put my
life
on hold
for you

i won't make
that mistake
twice

creamy crack

i thought
i loved you
but i didn't

you said you
were different
but you were really the same

you weren't lying though
you just thought you were different
but now you know

now we both do

i thought
i loved you
but i didn't

thank God

dried out

fighting to be heard
is a battle
i'll never win
with you
but the silence is
killing me

sharp edges

whoever said
words don't hurt
never met

you

your words cut
deeper
than any knife
ever could

bad weave

i love him
he loved me
things have changed as you can see
circumstances took away
the chance of us being together
didn't think it would last forever
but can't say i didn't wish on that cliche star
that i could live my days in his arms

i crossed my fingers
& my toes
& only the lord knows
how hard i tried
cried
& prayed
that he would let our love stay
i would close my eyes & wonder why
he couldn't manage to just do right

it's funny how we love
those we shouldn't love
so hard

but when something is not meant to be
you can make it be
but know you are sacrificing
the privilege of being happy

strong-hold

you know in movies when the guy gets injured
and he tells his friend “go on without me”
but the person comes back for them anyway

in the movie they typically both make it out
but that doesn’t happen in real life

in real life we don’t both make it out
i come back for you
i sacrifice myself for you
i don't make it out

and in my last moments i am wishing
i had just left you behind

not to die but to be someone elses project
someone else's heart break
heartache
and to put it unkindly
someone else's mistake

next time
i will choose me
i will go on without you
and i won't look back

pressed

you tear me to shreds
and call it love
you serenade me with your lies
and call it romance

and i fall for it

every
single
time

split ends

some
people
prefer
you
broken

petroleum

bandaids don’t heal
they protect
bandaids stop outside things from getting in

if you have a bandaid on your heart
how can love get in
how can you truly heal

sometimes protection can hinder healing
rip off the bandaid
take off the armor

i know
you could get hurt again

but maybe you won't this time
and wouldn't that be great

chemicals

i think the most toxic relationship
i've ever had

was the one i had with myself
i malnourished my soul
and neglected my mental health

constantly undervalued what
i had to offer
and accepted the lowest bid

got angry at folks for treating me
no better than i did

lowered expectations to meet
people where they were

loved boys that didn't love me
and was surprised when i got hurt

chemicals

i lied to myself
cried to myself
and tried to people please

i forgot about me
and put myself last every time

but that's over now
i broke up with the old me
and i'm never going back

dandruff

i can't believe
i let you knock me down

i can't believe
i let you step on me

but you'll get
what you give

and i'm stronger
'cause of it

you can't change me
you won't break me

the fall out

the debris settles & the damage is now visible
i am no longer blinded by the storm
the consequences of the choices i made
lay in front of me

i couldn't see past the feelings i had for you
i saw the signs but i couldn't
or wouldn't allow myself to believe them
even through the storm i held on to you

i stand here with bruises & scratches
while you are untouched

i was torn between loving you & protecting myself
but now i can see what my inability
to see through your lies caused

i search for something i can salvage
but all that's left is broken pieces
that i must find a way to put back together
this
is
the aftermath
of loving you

loss

loss

i search for you
i look but i cannot find
and each time i come up empty
a piece of me dies

i cry for you
i scream out your name
in hopes that you'll hear me
i pray for God to heal me
but i still ache
the pain is so fresh
like it all happened yesterday

i miss you
i run back in my mind
the things i would say
had i known i only had one more day
and no matter how hard try
or how loud i cry
nothing brings you back to me

thinning

some say living is harder than dying
and i believe this to be true
cuz while i watched you slip away from me
there was nothing i could do
you went to heaven
a better place, they say
while i stayed here on earth
ashes to ashes dust to dust they said
as they dropped you in the dirt
my heart was broken
and all i could feel was pain
you were my sunshine
in the midst of a storm
the rainbow after the rain
i thought of the days
when we laughed and played
and that was all there was
when we went to the zoo
museums and took long walks
just because

people come and go
that much i know
but i never really thought it would
be someone i loved

reflection

when she smiled
i smiled
when she laughed
i laughed
when she frowned
i frowned
when she slept
i slept
anything she did
i would do

so i cried
when she died
and when she died
something inside me died too

broken strands

i have others
i love others
but there is none other like you
so i'm stuck
trying to fill an unfillable void
that should be filled with you

i never understood how you could leave me
bc i always believed if you loved me
you would've stayed
so each night i prayed
for God to return you to me
but now i see
you had no choice in the matter

because if you did
i'd be laughing instead of crying
you'd be sitting next to me instead of watching over me
& i'd be complete instead of just being broken pieces

just know that i love you & i miss you
& that once we meet again we will be inseperable

know that because of you i am stronger
than i ever thought possible
and i am who i am all because you loved me

stripped

you once told me that no matter what
you'd always be there
so when you left
i searched for you...
in my dreams and in my reality
i looked in every nook and cranny for you
i cried for you because i missed you
fought not to forget you
i held on tight to every memory of you
afraid that if i let go, i'd lose you
and lose myself in the process

i am broken without you
you were my air and my lungs
i am choking without you
you were my missing pieces
i am incomplete and defeated without you
you were my everything
and i feel like nothing without you

thoughts of the times
i may have let you down haunt me
days i should've spent with you that i let slip away
moments i should've hugged you
or told you how much i loved you and i didn't
i can only hope you remember the times that i did
i wish someone had told me to cherish
every second with you, that one day you'd disappear

low manipulation

low manipulation

it is so much
sweeter
when you

love

from a place
of feeling

loved

twist out

in the midst of all the chaos i have one constant
one light at the end of the tunnel
assuring me there is an end to my struggle

one pair of eyes that i can see my smile in
two arms open to me then closing around me
to hold me tight at the end of a long day

a voice that soothes me & makes my stress disappear
the person that's beside me when i think i'm all alone
whose kisses take away my pain and
whose words can calm me
those eyes, lips, arms, words
that voice belongs to [you]

you are my constant
my ally in the trenches of war
my bridge across the lake of doubt and distrust
my crutches that help me along when i am too weak
to do it by myself

the railing i can lean on to keep from falling
the soft melody that eases my headache
and lulls me to sleep
the world is constantly changing
while in the most imporant ways you stay the same

moisturizer

i will be
a glass of water so you can drink me
a boat on the sea so you can sink me
a grain of sand
so u can build pyramids on egyptian lands

i will be
a cold pitcher of ice tea
to cool you off when u overheat

i will be
the icing on your cake
the nourishment on your plate
the words of wisdom that keep your
path straight
& the realness thats never fake

i will be
the waves in the ocean
the love in your potion
the smile in your eyes
your wings so you can fly
your inspiration so the dream inside of you
you can realize

moisturizer

i will be
the thought in your mind
that shows you what never waits is time

i will be
your heart to keep you on beat
your favorite song and keep you on your feet

your light in darkness so you can find your way
the kind words that get you through the day

i will be
the friend that never leaves you
the conscience that leads you
the hand that doesn't hesitate to feed you

but most importantly

i will be
there ...

silk wrap

this ain't no love poem
no release the doves poem
no holding hands on the beach
happily ever after
together for all time
type of rhyme

bc i am tired of those

even though my eyes light up when i see you
& all i want to do is breathe you
my heart skips beats
my stomach does summersaults
just at the thought of you and...
aht aht
this ain't no love poem

those are over done
and i for one
am tired of it

the happy endings
when that is not the end of it
only the tip of it
there's more to it you know
the highs and the lows
but if you can get through those...

silk wrap

the love can be sweet
& sweep you off your feet
like 90's r&b
but only if you want to be
swept & kept

& if you don't want to be
that's okay
because
this ain't no love poem
anyway

pre-poo

love comes with such
complication and consequence
i'd rather be in like
that's when everything is okay
the "no you hang up first" stage
when you walk around holding hands
& exchanging kisses
i miss those days

save your edges

so many women out here
are broken to pieces
because they are trying to make
some man do right by them
& i'm not judging because i've been there
but here is a tip that will
save you a lot of time and therapy

stop sacrificing your

sanity
joy
time
edges
youth
money
credibility
self esteem
self worth

your ---> self

save your edges

all for people
who don't care enough about you
to not make you sacrifice
those things in the first place

and that goes for everyone
not just some man
but anyone and everyone
save your edges baby

referral

this might
be for you ...

you

deserve

better

kinky curly

i struggled to love
myself
i cannot
i will not
struggle with you
or beg you
to love me too

quick trim

i let you go
and only then
did i grow

i trimmed you
like split ends

i thrived
you were swept away by the wind

i could have held onto you
but the growth would have been in vain

i would have looked different
but remained the same

now the damage is gone
its like you were never there
and
now
i can move on

new growth

new growth

who will love her when she doesn't love herself
when she doesn't recognize her own wealth
when she doesn't think she's worthy so she constantly worries
and the insecurities become like small rips in her stocking
unnoticeable at first
until they get worse
and there is nothing left but the hole

who will love her as she bends and breaks
moving boneless like a snake
working so hard to please others
that she forgets her own existence
when she looks in the mirror
and doesn't recognize her own reflection
who is this?

she watched the woman that came before her
undervalue herself
take on way too much and never ask for help
she picked up the habits the woman laid down
she tried them on one by one like beautiful ball gowns
they fit her all too well
so now she has no choice but to keep them

new growth

the weight of the world has been passed
down to her like an heirloom
casting a shadow so dark
she wouldn't dare bloom
a way of thinking she was doomed to inherit
she is now a parrot
speaking words that were once spoken to her
words that once broke her
doing things she swore to never repeat
she accepts defeat
because the trauma just runs too deep

she is now the woman
she looks down at the little girl
looking up at her for guidance
she doesn't have the strength
but she finds it
to break the chains so they can both be free
the curse will be broken
because the generations behind her need it to be

good hair

i might catch some flack for this
but i'mma tell it anyway

i used to wish i was white
to live a completely free life

with no strings intertwined into nooses attached
standing tall without my ancestors burdens on my back
and no comparisons to brown paper sacks

a life where i wasn't told
i could be anything i wanted to be
i was shown it
it was my birthright so i was born already knowin' it

i wished i was part of the majority
with all the authority
whose word was never second guessed
and could walk around a store
without being accused of theft

don't walk around with your hands
in your pockets
my grandma would say
they'll think you're stealin'
even though i'm just feelin'
for the money so i can pay

good hair

i wanted milk white skin so i could fit in
green or blue eyes so i could be beautiful like them
i wanted so badly for my hair to blow in the wind
but my curls were stubborn and stiff
& i'm ashamed to say i was that black girl
who couldn't wait to say what she was mixed with

you got that
good hair
what you mixed with?
i'd answer with a grin
black, white, & indian

i wasn't lying but
i took way too much pride in
diluting my blood line

but now?
whew chile...
now?!

you couldn't pay me to be anything other than

black black black black

and i'm so proud of the fact
that no amount would do
to make me switch places with you

hot comb

i wonder if
i hurt my mom
when i thought i was
less than
beautiful

i wonder if
when i called
myself
ugly
it cut her
as deeply as it cut me
did she bleed?

i wonder if my ancestors
rolled over in their graves
when i became a new type of slave

beating my curls into submission
asking for permission
to occupy spaces
they paved the way for
and knocked on doors
they bust down for me
long before
i was born

4c

they will tell you that she was
strong and unafraid
that she won every battle
and emerged unscathed

they will conveniently
leave out that
she too was broken
she too fell to her knees
with tears in her eyes
and sorrow in her soul
she too cried out for mercy

she was strong yes
because she was held to the fire
and forged by the flames
she was never unscathed
the scars were just so much a part of her
that no one could tell the difference
they were her armor but also
her story of triumph and victory

but they did not come without sacrifice
every battle
she paid the price
she had losses
they made the wins
that much sweeter

shrinkage

my curls shrink
i do not

i will not shrink into the box
that you have conveniently crafted for me

i will not shrink my vision
because you cannot see

i will not become smaller than what i am
to please or placate some man

i will not slink around
with my head hung low
you may not be aware of my worth
but trust that i know

i will not bury my dreams
i only plant seeds
and i will grow with them
wild and free

shrinkage

i cannot hide my gifts
to make you or anyone else more
comfortable

well... i could
but i can't
and i won't
i will forever refuse to
because i choose to

after all

my curls shrink
i do not

curl crush

someone thinks i'm beautiful
they love the bend in my smile
with my not so straight teeth
and the little dimple in my right cheek

they love the twists in my curls
the naps in my “kitchen”
and the black on my knees

they love the stretch marks
the stress marks and
my un-lotioned feet.

someone thinks i’m smart
and cool
and that i light up their day
someone thinks i’m cute when i’m pouting
because i didn’t get my way

curl crush

someone thinks i'm funny
and laughs at all my jokes
someone lifts me up when i have lost all hope

someone thinks i'm special
and i was put here for a reason
someone understands i'm not perfect
and loves me through every season.

we are taught to search for this someone
high and low and to never cease
well I've finally found that someone
and that someone
is
me

curl-friends

get you a friend
that challenges you
and that brings out
the best in you

that roots for you
loves you when
you have forgotten how
prays for you when
you can't find the words

a friend that pours into you
and one that you can pour into

a ride or fly
[we don't die over here]

a pick up where we left off
no matter how long it's been
type of curl-friend

curl-friends

friendship
sisterhood
is undervalued
but necessary

get you one
but be one too
because while you may be special
the world doesn't revolve around you

curl shine

i will never steal your shine
if anything
i will lend you some of mine

there is enough for the both of us

if you shine
i shine
we shine together

curl pattern

hey boo
you are beautiful too

i know you see that other girl
with hair down her back
and skin smooth as butta

i know you see how the men flock to her
and you wonder what's wrong with you

but...

her beauty doesn't
take away from you
her smile shouldn't steal your joy
she is not your competition
she is your reflection
she is not your enemy
she is your sister

and i promise you
you are beautiful too

the journey

how you love yourself will set the tone
for how you love others
and how you
allow
others to love you

if you don't love who you are
flaws and all
you won't expect
or fully accept
that level
of love from someone else

protective style

protective style

i am not broken
i am just temporarily
out of service

i will be back
when i'm done
filling my cup

and
not
a
second
sooner

because you know what they say
you can't pour from
an empty wine bottle

tutorials

so many times
we give
the advice
we should be
taking

one
more
time
for the people in the back

so many times
we give
the advice
we should be
taking

the root

find the root
of the trauma

then

rip it out

only then can you
truly

grow

hair trauma

by the way
you should
go to therapy

not that you're crazy
or anything

but even if you are (or aren't)
you should go
you are probably hurting in
places and in ways you don't even
understand

and if you ever
want to get better
i suggest you go

address the trauma
stop the drama
and move on

regimen

break

the cycle

or

the cycle

will

break

you

rinse + repeat

- figure out who you are
- never forget whose you are
- find your purpose
- operate in your purpose

diffuser

the world is
a little brighter
every
day
because
you
are in it

never forget that

satin pillowcase

all the likes
in the world

won't
make
you

love yourself

baby hair

we are life-makers
cycle breakers
breath takers
raising world shapers

we shake off the toxicity
embrace simplicity
all while loving ourselves
authentically

hot oil treatment

thank you to those that could have
turned their back on me
when i wasn't that great of a friend
sister
daughter
wife
mother
cousin
thank you
for charging it to my mind
& not my heart

well oiled

coconut oil ...

less
is
more ...

trust me

leave-in

some people will
love what you do

some will not

some will clap for you

some will
not

some will write your name on signs
show up every time
and cheer for you whether you win or lose

some will
not

some will believe in you

some
will
not

all that matters is
what category
you
fall
into

deep condition

i need you to do me a favor
i need you to forgive
& i need you to

heal

it is a lot to ask

i know

& i probably don't
have the right to ask you
for something so big
but I need you to heal
because you deserve it
and the world needs a
better you
and i think you do too

length check

keep pushing

keep creating

keep doing

keep going

keep hoping

keep dreaming

keep your head up

braid out

mirrors show you
how others
see you
but you should
never let it dictate
how
you
see
yourself

wide tooth comb

people are struggling
around you
they are hurting
in ways you can't see
and most of them
are struggling in

silence

be gentle
be kind
it literally costs you
nothing

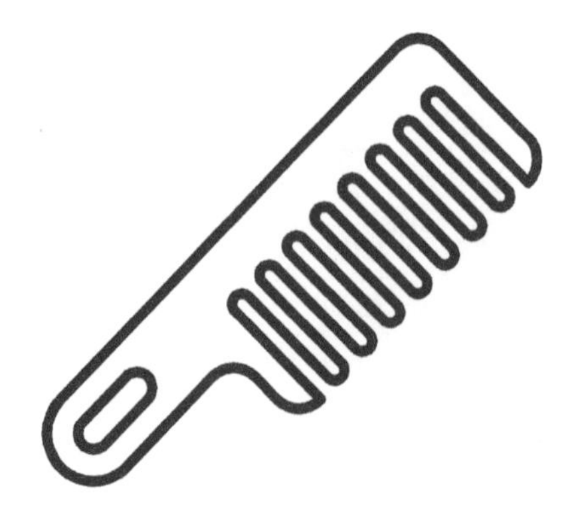

frizz

there are people
that don't like you

for no reason
literally no reason
absolutely positively no reason

that's crazy right?

well

now that you know
you can let it go
stop trying to figure it out

don't waste another minute of your time
or your energy

over processed

don't get so caught up in
rushing the process
that you miss
the beauty of it

and before you ask

yes
there is beauty
in the process

super grow

we we want to

fast forward
through the pain
the sadness
and the hurt

pause
all the good times
yet if we were to

rewind
we'd realize that the bad times
made the good times better

understand that
we go through
what we go through
so we can
grow through
the hardships

press
play

blow out

whew
Lord knows it is
not easy
doing what you do
but you constantly
make it through
and for that

i am
so
proud
of
you

detangle

when people are unfulfilled in their lives
or with themselves
they can't clap for you

they are unable to celebrate you
and be there for you
bc they are feeling empty
and are focused on
filling that void

everyone is not like that
but some people are

i have come to terms with it
i don't take it personal anymore

i keep it moving and wish them the best
jealousy rarely has anything to do with you
the quicker you learn that
the better off you'll be

bobby pins

people that don’t want
you to succeed
are just as important
to your journey
as those that do

they hold you up
just the same
they just don't know it

sulfate free

be for others
what others
couldn't be for you

the big chop

everyone wants things
to be fixed

but

no one wants
to deal with
the inconvenience of

construction

professional advice

my great grandma used to say
"a hard head makes
for a soft behind"
she didn't say "behind" though

and it is still one of the most
real statements
i've ever heard

i was little when she
first told me this
so i didn't get it

but i've learned how true
that statement is
the hard way

the transition

your time is coming
don't look around at
what everyone else is doing
or accomplishing
they had to
wait
for their chance
just like you

right now

clap for them
celebrate them
keep your head up
and keep moving
forward

treatment

you can be content without being complacent
you can be appreciative of what you have
while attempting to achieve more
you can be grateful for how far you've come
while still
trying to go further

the problem comes in when people get so
wrapped up
in getting what they want
that they take for granted
what they currently have

don't miss out on the beauty
of the present
of the now

pineapple method

your purpose is not for you
it is for others
someone needs
what God
has placed inside of
you
that's why it's so important
for you to
walk in it

wash and go

you are perfect
just the way you are
unless
you're like a serial killer
or something
in that case
you might need
to do something about that

wash day

i may not come
when you want me
& i probably
won't
be
on
time

i am not
God

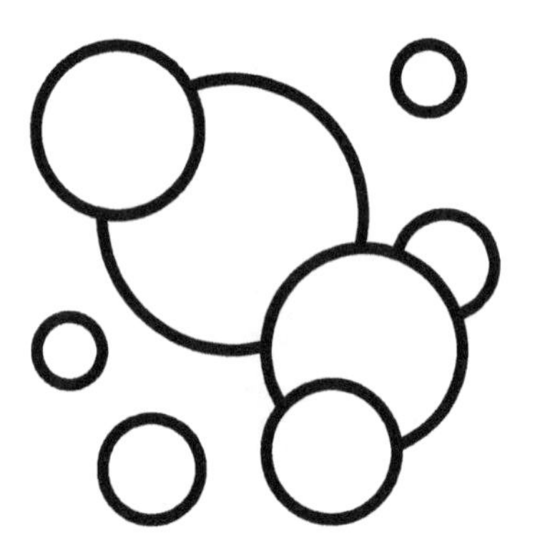

dry ends

if you're speaking
on someone else's
addictions without
acknowledging
your own...

either you are in denial
or you don't see
the irony

bounce back

remember that time
when you thought you
wouldn't make it
but then you did

you're still here
don't give up

because you've made
it through 100% of
everything you've been through
you
are
still
here

nappy glory

i can't help but laugh
at the fact that i thought
i was supposed to have it
all figured out
in my 20's

let's have a moment of silence
for my naivety
.
.
.
now let us all laugh together lol

flexi-rods

if someone won't
let you over
into their lane
create your own

disclaimer:
this is
not
driving advice

untamed

untamed

i am not a well behaved black woman
they are extinct
you picked them from the bushes
and hung them from the trees

their bones fertilized the soil
i am their seed

you broke their bodies
but you could not harness their souls
they run wild within me

i am their bloodline
through me they will be
free

black stands

it used to be wars were fought overseas
but now the one with the target on their back
looks just like me
it's a war on us
their guns cocked and loaded
and there is no justice ... just ... us

hands in the air with nowhere to run
they remind us that we kill each other to norm it
but it is genocide ain't no other word for it

they'll say the degradation of the black family
structure is to blame
they keep that same song on repeat
but who is snatching the fathers
out the homes and
killing our young men in the streets

your father is gone so you turn to the block
your family leanin on you
you gotta be the rock
time is running out tick tock

time is up
but what they didn't tell you
is the system is corrupt
it was never made for you
it is doing what it was built to do

exposure

running running running
bang
shot him down in the street like he didn't have no name
like he was an animal
when really they are
living free when they should be behind bars
no consequence
no suspense
this is not a thriller

'cause we all know how this one ends
we all know who loses and who wins
we can't breathe, we can't walk and we sure can't run
can't be in the house or a car cuz folks shootin us for fun

let's clap one time
for black on black crime
cuz you know someone is gonna bring it up
pour a little out the cup for the lost souls
for the ones that refuse to see
that a threat is not what we're trying to be
we just want to live like you and do what do you
without ending up in a body bag
we don't want justification we want justice
i'm tired of saying their names bc it hurts ... but i will
continue to say them anyway and i won't stop until
something...
everything changes

stop the madness

we live in a world where family doesn't mean much
where money is everything power is much more
& life is tough
where news reporters become death reporters
and kids become video recorders
playing back the actions they see day to day

when kids carry guns and shoot a few people
its only a phase
body after body pops up cuz bullets are a common disease
along with man made cancer and stds
mothers bury daughters and fathers bury sons
but theres no one else to blame cuz we're the only ones
we see murder and death on the news
but everyone just assumes
theres nothing they can do
unless its their child plastered on the tv screen
that's when they want everyone to hear their screams
but when it was someone elses kid in someone elses
neighborhood
it was all good

but we can prevent these tragedies
parents need to realize that their problems
trickle down to their kids
that a lack of guidance leads back to a lack of discipline
stop the violence stop the hatred stop lettin your
kids go to school and fight

stop the madness

if sally didn't hit sherry wouldn't have to hit back right?
so she could sit back and learn in school instead
bullyin her peers b/c of her fears of inadequacy
so if Sherry and Sally can learn Bobby and Billy can
learn too so they all have something in their heads
when mommy and daddy tuck them in their beds

so make sure your baby boy isn't still a boy at 40
instead of a man
especially black people need to take a stand
cuz we're not expected to succeed but we can

they think the problem is with us but society
breeds stick up boys, corner boys, street pharmacists,
& addicts that'll kill for a hit

and in hopes of keeping them down
they've never been told yes instead of no
so they resort to physical destruction
bc they are told that their emotional dysfunction
is beyond reconstruction so the construction that
could be done won't be
cuz nobody cares about the tears in the life of a young
black child but they'll gladly throw him in jail
so the spirit that was once strong can disintegrate
and he can dissipate into the long line of stereotypes
he's grown to fit into
cuz that's the world he was born into

stop the madness

lets start to believe in & support our race
we wonder why there is so much black on black crime
its cuz we don't take the time to understand our people

we cry out for peace
but how can we expect kids to know
what peace is when all we show them is war

they see the senseless bloodshed and they thirst
for more

but we can stop it
take the things we've been offered for decades
the philosophies of MLK
Malcolm X minus the any means necessary
unless the violent meaning has digressed

lean on God and not your own understanding
you'll see the difference it all makes and
the lives it won't take
although violence is a word its been a way of life
we have to all come together &
stop
the
madness

About The Author

Brianna Laren is a wife, mom, writer and filmmaker. Born in Maryland and raised in Washington D.C, she has been writing stories, poems, and plays since she was a child, although that was mostly gibberish. She is the author of Breebe's Brand New Baby Brother, Pretty Pretty Black Girl and Edge Control for the Soul.

She graduated from the illustrious North Carolina A&T State University, where she received a degree in a major completely unrelated to writing. However, she attributes attending an HBCU to helping mold her into the woman she is today (making the student loan debt almost worth it).

Brianna's purpose is to create stories, characters, and content that positively reflects and uplifts the black community. Her mission is to change the narrative one keystroke at a time.

www.BriannaLaren.com
Photo credit: Jodie Brim Photography